WE CAN READ about NATURE!™

If YOU HAD A TAIL

by CATHERINE NICHOLS

BENCHMARK BOOKS

MARSHALL CAVENDISH
NEW YORK

*With thanks to
Susan Jefferson, first grade teacher at Miamitown
Elementary, Ohio, for sharing her innovative teaching
techniques in the Fun with Phonics section.*

Benchmark Books
Marshall Cavendish Corporation
99 White Plains Road
Tarrytown, New York 10591
Website: www.marshallcavendish.com

Photo Research by Candlepants, Inc.

Cover Photo: *The National Audubon Society Collection / Photo Researchers, Inc.*,
Mark Boulton

The photographs in this book are used by permission and through the courtesy of:
The National Audubon Society Collection / Photo Researchers, Inc.: Jeff Lepore, 4; Toni
Angemayer, 5, 21, 28 (top); M.H. Sharp, 6 (top); Tim Davis, 6 (bottom), 16-17, 22
(bottom); Alan & Sandy Carey, 7 (right); Art Wolfe, 8; Steve Maslowski, 9; Phil A.
Dotson, 10; Mark Boulton, 12; G. Soury Jacana, 13 (top); David T. Roberts, 18, 27
(bottom); Jeanne White, 22 (top); Leonard Lee Rue III, 23; George Lepp, 24-25; Tom
McHugh, 26 (top, left), 26 (bottom); Carolyn A. McKeone, 26 (top, right); Sven Zellner,
27 (top); John M. Coffman, 28 (bottom). *Animals Animals:* Laidler K&S OSF, 7 (left);
Erwin & Peggy Bauer, 13 (bottom); Charles Palek, 14-15; Paul Freed, 19. *Australian
Picture Library / CORBIS:* 11. *Swanstock, Marcy Merrill / Image Bank:* 29.

Library of Congress Cataloging-in-Publication Data

Nichols, Catherine.
If you had a tail / by Catherine Nichols.
p. cm. – (We can read about nature!)
Includes index (p.32).
ISBN 0-7614-1251-4
1. Tail–Juvenile literature. [1. Tail.] I. Title. II. Series
QL950.6.N53 2001   591.4–dc21   00-049846

Printed in Italy

1 3 5 6 4 2

Look for us inside this book.

beaver	cow
crocodile	foal
fox	gecko
kangaroo	lizard
mare	monkey
opossum	peacock
porcupine	rattlesnake
stingray	zebra

If you had a tail, what kind would it be?
Would your tail be short?

A bobcat

4

Or long?

Would it be bushy?

An eastern gray squirrel

Or curly?

A Yorkshire pig

A giraffe

A pangolin

Or tufted?

Or plated?

7

If you had a tail, would you hang from a tree like these monkeys?

Long-haired spider monkeys

Or like this opossum?
An opossum's tail is scaly and
has no hair.
This helps the opossum hold on.

A young opossum

A kangaroo's tail is strong.
This kangaroo is resting on its tail.

An eastern gray kangaroo

When kangaroos hop,
they use their tails to balance.

Crocodiles have long, flat tails. When they swim, they move their tails from side to side.

A Nile crocodile

A stingray's tail is long and thin.

A blue-spotted stingray

Beavers use their tails as paddles.

Look at this tail.
But don't get too close.
It belongs to a rattlesnake.

A western diamondback rattlesnake

When a rattlesnake shakes the tip of its tail, it is sending a warning: "Go away, before I bite!"

If you had a tail,
would it be a weapon?
This tail is sharp!
It is covered with quills.
A porcupine in danger
will raise its quills and
swing its tail.
Watch out!

Don't catch this lizard by its tail.
It will break off.
In time, the tail will grow back.

A five-lined skink

This gecko stores fat in its tail.
If food is hard to find,
it will live off the fat in its tail.

An African fat-tailed gecko

If you had a tail, would it be made of feathers?
This male peacock is spreading his tail.
He wants to attract a mate.
"Look at me," he says.
"I am such a handsome fellow!"

Swish, swish!
A mare and her foal . . .

and
a cow . . .

flick their tails to chase away flies.

Zebras stand like this for a reason. They are brushing flies from each other's faces.

A long, bushy tail comes in handy on cold winter nights.

This fox has wrapped its tail around its body.

Now it is cozy and warm.

Tails come in many different shapes and sizes.

An Afghan hound

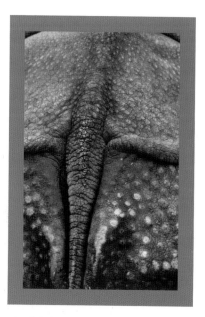

A rhinoceros

A sea horse

A chameleon

They can do all kinds of things.

Not every animal has a tail.
Chimpanzees don't.

Nor does this frog.

Nor, of course, do you.

fun with phonics

How do we become fluent readers? We interpret, or decode, the written word. Knowledge of phonics—the rules and patterns for pronouncing letters—is essential. When we come upon a word we cannot figure out by any other strategy, we need to sound out that word.

Here are some very effective tools to help early readers along their way. Use the "add-on" technique to sound out unknown words. Simply add one sound at a time, always pronouncing previous sounds. For instance, to sound out the word **cat**, first say **c**, then **c-a**, then **c-a-t**, and finally the entire word **cat**. Reading "chunks" of letters is another important skill. These are patterns of two or more letters that make one sound.

Words from this book appear below. The markings are clues to help children master phonics rules and patterns. All consonant sounds are circled. Single vowels are either long –, short ˘, or silent /. Have fun with phonics, and a fluent reader will emerge.

In short e words, the vowel e is sandwiched between consonants.

r ĕ d   h ĕ l p s   r ĕ s t i n g   g ĕ t

g ĕ c k ō

Bossy "er" says "rrr," as if something is growling.

ē a s t e r n   s p ī d e r   w ĕ s t e r n   c ŏ v e r e d
Rrrr   Rrrr   Rrrr   Rrrr

w i n t e r   d i f f e r e n t
Rrrr   Rrrr

30

Consonant clusters are two or three consonants in a group that make one sound when blended together.

s w ĭ m   f l ă t   c l ō s e   s h ā k e s

c h ĭ m p s   f l ĭ c k

Small sight words can be used as reading chunks when there are no other vowel rules to follow.

t h i n   h o l d   f a t   c o l d

f l a t   c a t c h   s t a n d   h a n d y ē

fun facts

- Beavers use their tails to warn other beavers of danger. If a beaver senses trouble, it slaps its tail on the water's surface. The sound can be heard throughout the woods.
- A kangaroo's tail is so strong it can support the animal's entire weight.
- Opossums carry leaves to their nests with their tails.
- After they lay their eggs, some crocodiles make nests in the sand with their tails.
- Only young five-lined skinks have bright blue tails. As they grow older, the tails fade to brown.
- Tadpoles need tails to swim. When a tadpole becomes a frog, the tail disappears.

glossary/index

about the author

Catherine Nichols has written nonfiction for young readers for fifteen years. She currently works as an editor for a small publishing company. She has also taught high-school English. Ms. Nichols lives in Jersey City, New Jersey, with her husband, daughter, and their pet Moonlight, a white cat with a long black tail.